MONEY MATTERS: A GUIDE TO FINANCIAL LITERACY

Everything You Need to Know About Money
in One simple-to-understand Guide

Daniel Davis

TABLE OF CONTENTS

PRESENTATION

Did you have at least some idea that only 33% of Americans have an adequate number of reserve funds to cover an unforeseen cost of $500? Financial literacy is a significant expertise that everybody needs to have to find true success and secure their future. In this book, we'll cover the nuts and bolts of financial literacy, including planning or budgeting, saving, money management, and that's only the tip of the iceberg. We'll likewise talk about the outcomes of not being financially literate, and the advantages of being financially literate. It gives you the basics and information you want to assume command or take control over your finances and make a solid future.

This book explains the different methods for saving money, such as setting up a savings account, using an automatic savings plan, and taking advantage of tax-advantaged savings accounts. It also discusses the importance of an emergency fund, and how to build an emergency fund.

In this book, we'll discuss the different types of investments, such as stocks, bonds, and mutual funds. Which explains the benefits and risks of each type of investment, and how to choose the right investments for your goals. Here's the section heading: "Investing 101: Understanding the Different Types of Investments". This section could provide tips on how to get started with investing, and how to develop a diversified portfolio.

Another section covers credit. This section explains the basics of credit, such as the difference between good and bad credit, and how to build and maintain good credit. It also explains the benefits and risks of using credit, and how to avoid common credit mistakes. Here's the section heading: "Understanding Credit: The Good, the Bad, and the Ugly". This section also includes tips on how to check your credit report, and how to fix any errors you find.

Chapter 1

MONEY MAKEOVER: A-STEP-BY STEP GUIDE TO GETTING YOUR FINANCE IN ORDER

Are you ready to take control of your finances and create a brighter future for yourself and your family? This chapter will provide you with a step-by-step guide to getting your finances in order. We'll start by assessing your current financial situation, and then we'll create a personalized plan to help you achieve your financial goals. We'll cover everything from budgeting and debt reduction to investing and financial protection. So, if you're ready to take charge of your finances. But before we get started I wish you to ask yourself some questions and answer them sincerely to yourself! What's your monthly income?Do you have any debt?What are your financial goals?.

Here are the steps in getting your finances in order.

Setting a clear financial goal is the initial step to setting your funds up. It's vital to pick a particular, quantifiable, and a feasible objective. For instance, your goal could be to save $5,000 for an emergency fund account before the year's over, or to pay off $10,000 of debt in a half year. It's also important to choose a goal that is relevant to your current situation and that you are passionate about.

Another SMART method is a great way to set a clear financial goal. The acronym stands for specific, measurable, attainable, relevant, and time-bound. Let's look at an example of how this might work for you. If your goal is to pay off $10,000 of debt, that would be specific, measurable, and time-bound. You could then break this goal down into smaller steps, like making an extra $200 per month toward your debt, or reducing your spending by $300 per month.

- **CREATE A BUDGET**

Create a budget, This means tracking your income and expenses and figuring out where your money is going. Once you have a good understanding of your finances, you can start to make changes. One important change is to reduce your expenses. This could mean finding ways to save on your grocery bill, cutting down on entertainment costs, or canceling unnecessary subscriptions. It could also mean finding ways to increase your income, such as getting a raise or starting a side hustle.

Making a financial plan or creating a budget is really more straightforward than you could naturally suspect! The initial step is to make a rundown of all your month to month pay and costs. You can utilize a bookkeeping sheet or an internet planning device to do this. Then, you'll need to isolate your costs into classifications, like lodging, food, transportation, and entertainment. Then, at that point, you'll have to decide your fundamental costs, similar to lease and utilities, and your unnecessary costs, such as eating out and amusement. At long last, you'll need to set a reasonable spending plan for every class, in view of your pay and your objectives.

- **STICK TO IT**

After you've created a budget, the next step is to stick to it! This can be the most difficult part, but there are some strategies that can help. One strategy is the "envelope method", where you use physical envelopes to keep track of your spending. Another strategy is the "pay yourself first" method, where you put money into savings as soon as you get paid. You can also try using a budgeting app to track your expenses and set goals.

There are a couple of things you can do to assist yourself with sticking to your budget or plan. In the first place, it's important to track your progress and reward yourself for sticking to your budget.You can likewise try automating your finances, so that your money is automatically transferred to savings or debt payments.

Finally, it's important to be flexible with your budget, as unexpected expenses can come up. If you find yourself struggling to stick to your budget, try reassessing your goals and making adjustments as needed.

- **TRACK YOUR PROGRESS AND MAKE ADJUSTMENTS AS NEEDED**

Tracking your progress and making adjustments is a key part of reaching your financial goals. It's essential to keep track of your development consistently, so you can perceive that you are so near arriving at your goals and make any important changes. For instance, you could check in with your advancement consistently, and survey your spending plan to check whether there are any regions where you can scale back. Then, at that point, on the off chance that you're not on target to arrive at your goal, you can make the fundamental changes or adjustments.

 There are multiple ways you can track your progress toward your financial goals. The first is to make a bookkeeping sheet to follow your spending and progress toward your objective. On the other hand, you could utilize a planning application to follow your spending and progress. Another choice is to record your advancement in a diary or journal. It's critical to pick a technique that works for yourself and that you will really utilize.

- **BUILD UP AN EMERGENCY FUND**

 Building up an emergency fund is a significant piece of arriving at your financial goals. An emergency fund is a reserve money that you can use for unforeseen costs, similar to an employment cutback or a health related crisis. It's prescribed to have an emergency fund that covers 3-6 months of everyday costs. To develop your emergency fund, you could begin by saving a specific measure of cash every month. For instance, you could set up a programmed move from your financial records to your bank account every month.

There are a few different ways you can build up your emergency fund, depending on your situation. One option is to start small, like setting aside $50 per month. You can gradually increase this amount as your budget allows. Another option is to use your tax refund or work bonus to boost your emergency fund. Another way to build up your emergency fund is to sell items you no longer need, like clothes, books, or furniture.

One strategy for paying off high-interest quickly is known as the "snowball technique". This technique includes making least installments on the entirety of your obligations aside from the one with the most noteworthy financing cost. You then, at that point, make additional installments on the obligation with the most elevated loan cost until it is paid off. When that obligation is paid off, you take the cash you were paying on that obligation and apply it to the following most noteworthy premium obligation. This goes on until every one of your obligations are paid off.

- **SET YOURSELF UP FOR LONG-TERM FINANCIAL SUCCESS BY INVESTING AND PLANNING FOR RETIREMENT**

Effective money management and making arrangements for retirement is a significant piece of long haul monetary achievement. The initial step is to decide your investment goals.For example, you might want to save for retirement, college, or a down payment on a house. Once you have identified your goals, you can create an investment plan to reach them. This plan could incorporate saving a specific measure of cash every month for your objectives, picking ventures that line up with your objectives, and reconsidering your arrangement as your life altering events.

There are a few key steps you can take to set yourself up for long-term financial success.

First, you should set up a retirement account, like a 401(k) or IRA(. 401(k) and IRA are both types of retirement accounts. 401(k) stands for "401(k) plan," and it's a retirement account that's offered by some employers. IRA stands for "Individual Retirement Account," and it's a retirement account that you can open on your own. Both types of accounts allow you to save money for retirement, and they both have tax benefits.). Next, you should determine how much money you need to save for retirement and how much you can afford to save each month. Then, you should invest your money in a diversified portfolio that includes stocks, bonds, and other assets. You should also consider your risk tolerance and time horizon when choosing investments. Finally, you should review your plan periodically and make adjustments as needed.

CHAPTER 2

BUDGETING FOR RAINY DAY: HOW TO SAVE FOR EMERGENCIES

Having an emergency fund is one of the main pieces of financial planning. An emergency fund can assist you with enduring unforeseen financial storms, similar to employment misfortune, clinical expenses, or home fixes. In this section, we'll go over all that you want to be familiar with building a rainy day account or emergency fund, including how much cash to save and how to work out that sum. We'll likewise examine the advantages of having a rainy day account and how it can give you genuine serenity and financial security.

An emergency fund is a save or reserve of cash that you put away for unexpected expenses. It's not the same as a bank account since it's particularly for crises, similar to an unexpected employment cutback or a startling hospital expense. Having an emergency fund gives you a monetary wellbeing net that can assist you with overcoming difficult stretches without venturing into the debts. A rainy day account ought to be effectively available, so you can get to it rapidly when you really want it. It's likewise vital to ensure your emergency fund is liquid, meaning it's in a bank account or another record that you can get to without any problem.

 Having an emergency fund is significant for a couple of reasons. To start with, it can assist you with trying not to venture into debt in case of an emergency. Without an emergency fund, you could need to utilize a Visa or apply for a new line of credit to cover unforeseen expenses. This can lead to high-interest debt that's difficult to pay off. Second, an emergency fund can give you genuine serenity, realizing that you have a pad to return to in case of a crisis. Lastly, a secret stash can assist you with keeping focused with your other monetary objectives, such as putting something aside for a home or retirement.

 An emergency fund is significant, however there are a couple of normal mix-ups to stay away from. One error isn't having a particular goal for your emergency fund. Without an objective, it's difficult to tell how much cash you want to save.

Another mix-up is keeping your emergency fund in a regular saving account. These records commonly have low loan fees, so your cash will not develop however much it could. A third mistake is not having an arrangement for getting to your emergency. On the off chance that you don't have an arrangement for getting to your assets, you might wind up involving them for non-emergency expenses.

When building an emergency fund, it's important to consider your individual circumstances. For example, if you have a stable job and other sources of income, you may not need as large of an emergency fund as someone with a more variable income. If you have children or dependents, you'll also need to factor in their needs when deciding how much to save. And finally, your personal comfort level is also important. Some people feel more secure knowing they have a large emergency fund, while others are comfortable with a smaller amount.

It's additionally critical to consider the potential dangers you might confront while choosing the amount to save. For instance, on the off chance that you're in a high-risk calling, similar to development or policing, might need to have a bigger emergency fund.

Or if you live in an area prone to natural disasters, you might need to have more cash put away. Furthermore, in the event that you have an ailment that could prompt costly doctor's visit expenses, it means a lot to anticipate that. Here is the list of common types of emergencies that an emergency fund can cover:

1.Job loss:

In the event that you experience employment loss, having an emergency fund can assist you with covering your costs until you secure another position. It's essential to ensure your emergency fund can cover something like three to six months of everyday costs. This can give you an opportunity to get another line of work without stressing over how to take care of your bills. During this time, you may likewise need to consider different types of revenue, such as outsourcing or selling things on the web. What's more, remember to apply for joblessness bebebenefits.

2.Theft or burglary:

In case of a robbery or thievery, your emergency fund can assist with taking care of the expense of replacing taken things or fixing any harm to your home. It's essential to have a precise stock of your assets, so you can without much of a stretch figure out what should be supplanted. You ought to likewise really look at your insurance contracts to ensure you're shrouded if there should arise an occurrence of robbery or theft. Furthermore, remember to do whatever it may take to safeguard your home and possessions, such as introducing security frameworks or locking your entryways and windows.

3.Pet medical expenses

An emergency fund can likewise be a lifeline with regards to pet clinical expenses. Veterinary bills can be costly, and it's critical to be ready for any unexpected expenses. Notwithstanding your backup stash, you may likewise need to think about pet protection. Pet insurance can assist with taking care of the expense of veterinary consideration, meds, and, surprisingly, pet incineration or even enentombment.

4.Travel emergencies

Travel emergencies can likewise put a strain in your funds. Assuming you need to drop or change your itinerary items because of an emergency, your emergency fund can assist with taking care of the expenses. You may likewise need to consider travel protection, which can give inclusion to things like flight undoings, lost baggage, or health related crises while voyaging. Furthermore, remember to explore the tourism warnings for your objective and buy any essential immunizations or prescriptions.

5. Natural disasters

Natural disasters like hurricanes, earthquakes, and wildfires can also cause significant financial strain. In addition to your emergency fund, you may want to consider purchasing disaster insurance, which can provide coverage for things like damage to your home and belongings. You ought to likewise have a crisis plan set up, including an assigned gathering spot and supplies like food, water, and emergency treatment units. And don't forget to consider your pets - have a plan in place for evacuating with your furry friends.

6. Legal Issue

Legal issues can be unbelievably distressing and exorbitant. On the off chance that you end up confronting a legal issue, your emergency fund can assist with covering things like lawyer expenses and court costs. You ought to likewise have a decent comprehension of your legitimate freedoms and responsibilities.Having an essential comprehension of the law and being know about your limitations can have a major effect on the off chance that you at any point face a lawful issue.

Furthermore, remember to think about your protection inclusion - for instance, property holder's protection might give an inclusion to legitimate defense costs.

7. Loss of loved one

Losing a friend or family member is a troublesome and close to home insight. It can likewise have a huge monetary effect. Burial service costs can be costly, and there might be other unforeseen expenses related with a passing, as legitimate charges or travel costs. Your emergency fund can assist with taking care of these expenses and give you some monetary security during this troublesome time. It's likewise vital to be ready for the profound effect of losing a friend or family member.

It's critical to consider every one of the reasonable and monetary parts of losing a friend or family member, however zeroing in on your own close to home prosperity is similarly significant. Melancholy is a characteristic interaction, and everybody encounters it in an unexpected way. Certain individuals track down solace in conversing with others, while others like to keep their contemplations hidden. There is no set in stone manner to lament, however it's critical to be aware of your own requirements and deal with yourself.

8. Business losses

Losing a business can be wrecking, both financially and emotionally. Business misfortunes can occur for various reasons, as monetary slumps, catastrophic events, or unfortunate administration choices. At the point when a business comes up short, there can be critical monetary misfortunes, including the deficiency of individual resources. An emergency fund can assist with relaxing the blow of a business misfortune, but at the same time having other monetary shields set up, similar to insurance, is significant.

There are a couple of things you can do to get ready for the chance of a business misfortune. One is to differentiate your pay sources, so that assuming one type of revenue is lost, you have others to return to. It's additionally essential to have a leave procedure set up, in the event that you really want to close down your business. This could incorporate selling your business, slowing down tasks, or moving possession.

CHAPTER 3

A PERSONAL FINANCE GUIDE FOR MILLENNIALS

With regards to individual finance, twenty to thirty year olds face remarkable difficulties and open doors. With the right financial strategies, they can get themselves positioned for long haul achievement. This section will give a complete manual for individual accounting for recent college grads, covering planning, obligation to the executives, money management, and more. By heeding the guidance and procedures in this part,millennials can take control of their finances and achieve their financial goals.

The main thing to remember is that millennials face unique financial challenges, like higher student loan debt and lower wages. This can make it hard to put something aside for the future and arrive at monetary objectives. However, there are additionally extraordinary open doors for millennials, similar to the potential for higher profit from now on.

The millennial age, brought into the world somewhere in the range of 1981 and 1996,faces unique challenges and opportunities when it comes to

personal finance . Twenty to thirty year olds grew up during the Incomparable recession, a period of economic uncertainty, and they have been molded by the computerized age. They are frequently burdened with educational loan obligations and face stagnant wages. In any case, they likewise approach more monetary devices and assets than any past age. This part will investigate the monetary scene for twenty to thirty year olds, and give common sense counsel and procedures to making monetary progress. There are a variety of topics this chapter covers, including!

- Personal finance

Personal finance is the management of your money and assets, including your income, spending, savings, and investing.
It's a way to take control of your financial future and achieve your goals. Personal finance is the most common way of dealing with your cash and settling on brilliant monetary choices. It incorporates planning, saving, money management, and the sky's the limit from there. One of the most vital phases in individual finance is to figure out your ongoing monetary

circumstance. This means taking a close look at your income, expenses, assets, and debts. . When you have a reasonable image of your funds, you can begin making an arrangement to work on your monetary wellbeing.

There are a few key things to keep in mind when making financial decisions. First, make sure you're considering the long-term consequences of your choices. It's easy to get caught up in the moment and make a decision that's not in your best interest in the long run. Second, don't be afraid to seek help from a financial professional. They can provide guidance and support as you make important decisions. Finally, remember that financial decisions are often emotional. Take the time to think through your choices and be honest with yourself about your priorities.

- Creating a budget

Creating a budget or making a financial plan can appear to be overwhelming, however it doesn't need to be. The initial step is to accumulate the entirety of your monetary data, including pay stubs, bank statements and bills. When you have all of your data in a single spot, you can begin to classify your costs. This incorporates fixed costs, similar to lease and utilities, and variable costs, similar to food and diversion. When you have a decent comprehension of where your cash is going, you can begin to make an arrangement for how to dispense your cash in a manner that lines up with your objectives.

While making a financial plan, one of the main interesting points is your needs. What are the main things to you, and how would you like to appropriately designate your cash? For instance, in the event that you're attempting to put something aside for a major purchase, similar to a house, you might need to focus on saving over different costs. Or then again, assuming you're attempting to take care of obligation, you might need to focus on obligation reimbursement over different objectives. Understanding your needs will assist you with making a spending plan that works for you.

Whenever you've identified your priorities or needs and sorted your costs, now is the right time to make your financial plan. There are a couple techniques you can use to make a spending plan. The 50/30/20 rule is a well known strategy that separates your costs into three classifications: 50% for needs, 30% for needs, and 20% for investment funds. There's likewise the zero-based planning strategy, where you designate each dollar of your pay to a specific category.

- Managing credit card debt

Credit card debt is money that you owe on your credit cards. This can happen when you utilize your charge cards to make buys and don't take care of the equilibrium in full every month. The loan fees on charge cards are much of the time high, which can make it hard to take care of the debt.Credit card debt can have a negative impact on your credit score and can make it harder to get approved for loans in the future.

Credit card debt can be a significant source of financial stress, yet there are ways of overseeing it and refocusing. The first step is to create a plan to pay off your debt. This might include laying out an objective to take care of your debt in a specific measure of time, similar to two years. Then, at that point, you can deal with diminishing your spending and expanding your pay to arrive at your goal.

The next stage in dealing with your credit card debt is to make a spending plan. This includes following your spending and distinguishing regions where you can scale back. For instance, you might need to lessen your spending on eating out, amusement, or dress. Whenever you've made a spending plan, the following stage is to adhere to it! This can be troublesome, yet keeping fixed on your objective of taking care of your debt is significant.

Since you have a spending plan, another step is to increase your income or to build your pay. This can assist you with taking care of your obligation quicker and arrive at your objective sooner. There are one or two methods for expanding your pay, including requesting a raise, getting a more lucrative line of work, or beginning a part time job

- **Investing for the future**

Investing is a significant part of individual finance, and it can assist you with arriving at your drawn out financial objectives. The initial step is to define an objective for your ventures, such as putting something aside for retirement or an up front installment on a house. Then, you'll have to pick the right sort of venture account, similar to a 401(k) or IRA. At last, you'll have to choose the right ventures for your record, similar to stocks, bonds, or mutual funds.

1. A stock fund is a type of investment that permits you to purchase a little piece of proprietorship in an organization or company. At the point when you put resources into a stock fund, you're basically purchasing a portion of the asset, which thus possesses portions of various organizations. The worth of the asset will go up or down contingent upon the presentation of the organizations it holds. Stock fund can be an effective method for enhancing your portfolio and reducing risk.

2. A bond fund is a type of investment that permits you to put resources into various bonds. These can incorporate government securities, corporate securities, or metropolitan securities. At the point when you put resources into a security reserve, you're crediting cash to the element that gave the bonds, and you'll get revenue installments consequently. The fundamental benefit of bond funds is that they will generally be less unstable than stock assets,

making them a decent choice for consecutive investors.

3. A mutual fund is a type of investment that permits you to pool your cash with different financial investors to buy a collection of protections, like stocks, bonds, or different resources. This implies that you'll get the advantage of enhancement without purchasing and deal with an enormous number of individual protections. There are various kinds of common assets, including file reserves, which track a particular record like the S&P 500; deadline reserves, which are intended for retirement financial backers; and effectively overseen reserves, which are overseen by professional fund directors.

- **Protecting your finance with insurance**

In simple terms, insurance is a way to protect yourself financially from the unexpected. You pay a premium, or a fee, to an insurance company, and in exchange, the company agrees to pay for specific losses or damages that are covered by your policy. For example, if you have car insurance, the insurance company will pay to repair your car if you're in an accident. Or, if you have health insurance, the insurance company will pay for your medical bills if you get sick or injured.

Insurance is a significant piece of safeguarding your funds. There are various kinds of insurance, such as health insurance, car insurance, and life insurance. Health care insurance can assist with taking care of the expense of clinical consideration, vehicle insurance can assist with taking care of the expense of fixes or substitution after a mishap or accident, and life insurance can give a monetary security net to your family in the event that you pass on.

Kinds of insurance

1. Health insurance: is one of the most common types of insurance. It can help cover the cost of doctor visits, hospital stays, and prescription drugs. Most people get health insurance through their employer, but you can also buy it on your own.

2. car insurance: This can cover the cost of repairing or replacing your car if it's damaged in an accident.

3. Life insurance: This gives financial benefits to your family or different recipients on the off chance that you die. There are two primary sorts of life insurance: term disaster protection and entire life insurance. Term life insurance covers you for a particular time frame, similar to 10 or 20 years, and it's normally the more reasonable choice. Entire disaster insurance covers you for as long as you can remember, and it can likewise fabricate cash esteem after some time.

4. homeowners insurance: This can help cover the cost of repairing or rebuilding your home if it's damaged by a covered event, like a fire or a storm. It can also help cover the cost of replacing your belongings if they're damaged or stolen. And, it can provide liability coverage if someone is injured on your property.
Though there are other kinds or types of insurance.

- **Estate planning and creating a will**

Estate planning and making a will are significant pieces of safeguarding your funds or finances and your loved ones. Estate planning is the method involved with making arrangements for the administration and dissemination of your resources after you die or you're no more. This can incorporate making a will, setting up trusts, and picking a full legal authority.

A will is an authoritative record that frames your desires for how your resources will be conveyed after you pass on. It's essential to have a will, regardless of whether you have a ton of resources, so your family doesn't need to think about what you would have needed.

There are a few different ways to go about estate planning and creating a will. You can work with an estate planning attorney to create a customized plan, or you can use online resources to create your own will. If you're working with an attorney, they'll likely ask you questions about your assets, your family, and your wishes. Then, they'll create a plan and documents that are tailored to your needs. If you're creating a will on your own, there are many online resources that can guide you through the process.

CHAPTER 4

MONTEREY PLANNING FOR SELF-EMPLOYED

Monetary planning for the self-employed presents special challenges and opportunities. Without a traditional employer, the independently employed should assume responsibility for their own monetary future. This can be both energizing and overwhelming, yet with cautious preparation and the right strategies, it tends to be fulfilling and satisfying. This part will investigate the monetary arranging process for the independently employed, from understanding income to setting up a retirement plan. With the right preparation, the independently employed can have high expectations about their monetary future.

Self-employed people might find it challenging to foresee their pay from one month to another, as it can fluctuate in view of various variables. To make an income plan, following pay and costs after some time is significant. This can be done by setting up a system for tracking income and expenses, like using a spreadsheet or financial software. There are few topics we could chat about in this chapter!

- **Importance of separating business and individual finance**

This is vital for keeping up with accurate financial records and guaranteeing that all costs of doing business are properly tracked and deducted. Separating business and individual finance is crucial for various reasons.   In the first place, it makes it simpler to follow business pay and costs, which is significant for charge and monetary arranging purposes.

Second, it can assist with shielding your own resources from business liabilities.

Third, it can make it simpler to apply for business advances or different sorts of supporting.

Fourth, it can assist you with keeping an unmistakable qualification between your own and proficient lives.

A good next step is to foster a framework for dealing with your funds. This could incorporate utilizing programming like QuickBooks or a bookkeeping sheet program like excel. This will assist you with monitoring your pay and costs, and ensure that everything is appropriately classified. Another tip is to be steady in your record keeping. This will make it more straightforward to monitor your funds over the long haul and spot any patterns or trends.

Another important aspect of separating business and personal finances is tax planning. . You'll should know about the different assessment suggestions for your business and individual pay. For instance, you might be qualified for various derivations or credits in view of your business structure. You'll likewise have to monitor your business pay and costs all through the year to ensure you're ready for charge season.

There are a few steps to take to separate business and personal finances. To begin with, you'll have to open a different ledger or bank account for your business. This will make it more straightforward to follow business pay and costs. Then, you'll have to make separate bookkeeping records for your business and individual finances. At long last, you'll have to ensure that your deals are all made utilizing your business financial balance and that your own exchanges are all made utilizing your own Bank account.

Now that we've covered the essentials of isolating business and individual finances, we can discuss a few prescribed procedures. To start with, it's critical to routinely audit your funds. This will assist you with getting any missteps or errors almost immediately. Second, it's vital to have a backup plan if there should be an occurrence of a crisis. This could incorporate a just-in-case account or business protection. At long last, it's essential to remain coordinated and try not to blend your funds.

- **Importance of creating a business plan**

A business plan is a record that frames the objectives, systems, and monetary projections for a business. It's a fundamental apparatus for any entrepreneur, as it assists you with outlining your way to progress. A business plan ought to incorporate data about your organization's central goal, items or administrations, target market, monetary projections, from there, the sky is the limit. It's essential to make a business plan regardless of whether you're an independent business person or specialist.

Creating a business plan doesn't have to be a daunting task. Here's a

step-by-step guide:
1. Define your business and your goals.
2. Research your market and competitors.
3. Create a marketing plan.
4. Outline your financial projections.
5. Write an executive summary.
6. Review and revise your plan.
Remember, your business plan is a living document that can and should be updated as your business evolves.

Creating a business plan is significant in light of multiple reasons. In the first place, it assists you with explaining your business thought and objectives.

Second, it compels you to properly investigate things and figure out your market.

Third, it assists you with getting financing from financial backers or moneylenders.

Fourth, it assists you with fostering a guide for progress.

Fifth, it fills in as a kind of perspective point as you explore the highs and lows of maintaining a business.

There are a few extra advantages of making a business plan that are worth focusing on. To begin with,it can help you stay accountable and focused on your goals.

Second, it can assist you with recognizing possible issues or difficulties before they emerge.

Third, it can assist you with assessing your headway and make changes on a case basis.

Lastly, it can assist you with building a more grounded group by obviously imparting your vision and objectives.

- **by Getting a professional advice**

Getting professional advice can be an important part of the business planning process. This could include consulting with a lawyer, accountant, or other business professional who can help you navigate the legal and financial aspects of starting and running a business. This kind of advice can be invaluable, especially if you're new to business ownership.

One significant consideration while getting professional advice is tracking down the right consultants for your business. You'll need to find somebody who has insight in your industry and who you feel open to working with. It's likewise critical to find somebody who will pay attention to your thoughts and objectives and give genuine input.

There are a few justifications for why it's critical to get professional advice as you make your field-tested strategy. To begin with, it can assist you with staying away from exorbitant missteps.

Second, it can assist you with ensuring your business is set up legitimately and monetarily.

Third, it can give you inner harmony realizing that you have the help of specialists as you push ahead with your business.

Lastly, it can save you investment that you can zero in on different parts of your business.

CHAPTER 5

WHY FINANCIAL LITERACY IS BASIC FOR YOUR SUCCESS

One of the most important reasons to understand personal finance is that it can help you build wealth over time. By making smart choices about your money, you can make a monetary arrangement that permits you to save and contribute for your future. Regardless of whether you start with a limited quantity of cash, the force of self multiplying dividends can assist you with arriving at your objectives. Moreover, by keeping away from normal monetary errors, you can save yourself time, cash, and stress over the long haul.

There are several reasons why it's important to have a solid understanding of personal finance. In the first place, it can assist you with pursuing better monetary choices. With a solid groundwork of information, you'll have the option to make informed options about your money and your future.
Second, it can assist you with accomplishing your goals. Whether you need to put something aside for a

home, begin a business, or basically have a real sense of reassurance in your monetary circumstance, it is fundamental to figure out an individual budget.

Third, it can assist you with keeping away from monetary issues not too far off.

Financial literacy can help you achieve things like!

- **Financial Independence or freedom**

Financial literacy is quite possibly the main figure accomplishing monetary freedom. By understanding the basics of individual accounting, you can pursue choices that will put you on the way to autonomy. One of the main parts of monetary freedom is having a very much arranged financial plan. With a spending plan, you can follow your spending, set aside cash, and put forth monetary objectives. Also, monetary education can assist you with pursuing savvy speculation choices and create financial stability over the long run.

- **Understanding the power of compound interest**

Another important aspect of financial literacy is understanding the power of compound interest. Compound interest is the interest earned on the interest you've already earned. Over time, this can lead to exponential growth in your wealth. For example, if you invest $100 a month for 30 years with an average annual return of 7%, you'll end up with over $170,000! This is just one example of how compound interest can help you achieve financial independence.

To fully understand the power of compound interest, it's important to understand the difference between simple interest and compound interest. Simple interest is the interest that is earned on the original principal amount of money. On the other hand, compound interest is the interest that is earned on both the original principal and the accumulated interest. So, with compound interest, your money can grow at an increasing rate over time.

- **Home ownership**

Financial literacy can assume a urgent part in assisting you with accomplishing house buying. To start with, it's critical to comprehend your credit score and what it can mean for your capacity to get a home loan. With a good credit score, you'll have the option to fit the bill for a lower loan fee on your credit, which can save you a lot of cash over the existence of the credit. Likewise, financial literacy can assist you with planning for an initial investment and shutting costs. It can likewise assist you with dealing with your funds once you become a property holder.

As well as understanding your financial assessment and planning for an initial investment, one more significant part of financial literacy for house purchasing is grasping your relationship of debt to salary after taxes. This is the level of your month to month pay that goes towards taking care of your obligations. Moneylenders will utilize this proportion to decide the amount you can bear to acquire. By keeping your relationship of outstanding debt to take home pay low, you'll have a superior possibility being supported for a home loan.

- **A comfortable retirement**

One of the main objectives of monetary proficiency is to accomplish a comfortable retirement. To do this, beginning saving and contributing for retirement however right on time as possible may be significant. The previous you start, the additional time your cash needs to develop through the force of self multiplying dividends. Furthermore, it's vital to comprehend the various kinds of retirement accounts and the tax reductions they offer.

There are some genuine instances of how an absence of financial literacy had unfortunate results. One model is the 2008 financial crisis. During this time, many individuals lost their homes and reserve funds because of an absence of understanding about the dangers implied in subprime contracts and other complex monetary items.
 Another model is student loan debt. Many individuals are battling to take care of their understudy loans since they didn't completely comprehend the agreements of their credits when they took them out.

Dangers of not being financially literate
Coming up next are a portion of the risks of not having financial literacy:
- Acquiring cash at exorbitant loan costs
- Getting into Mastercard obligation
- Going with unfortunate venture choices
- Neglecting to make arrangements for crises
- Not putting something aside for retirement
- Not grasping your protection inclusion
These are just some of the many dangers of not being financially literate. By educating yourself about personal finance, you can avoid these dangers and make better decisions for your financial future.

www.ingramcontent.com/pod-product-compliance
Lightning Source LLC
Chambersburg PA
CBHW070224260726
48658CB00006BA/2155